I0417471

Women's Thought Guide To Pre-Nuptial Agreements

By pro-women advocate
V. Kittington

Published by V. Kittington
www.valkittington.com

Women's Thought Guide to Pre-Nuptial Agreements
Written by pro-women advocate V. Kittington

ISBN 978-1542323321

Printed and bound in the United States of America

This book is dedicated to the women mistreated and betrayed by their men.

TABLE OF CONTENTS

THINKING OVER WHERE YOU ARE IN THE DEAL

As the Perfectionist woman, you are likely to do really well or to marry really well or both with or without a child from a previous relationship. This book will help you if the great guy is too far gone in over-thinking matters.

You do not want to be dissuaded from getting married by a pre-nuptial agreement. You want to pre-negotiate a deal OR change the law in your State to set a minimum settlement despite a pre-nuptial or any agreement before getting married.

If you have met a great guy that happens to be wealthy while you were a go-go dancer, his favorite waitress, or a secretary, or just a person that made his eyes glimmer, there does need to be a path forward for you if the relationship does not 'stick'. His perspective is that he is advised by *his* lawyers and protecting himself from bad motives but that has nothing to do with you and it is not your problem.

Your problem as a woman is that you will be swept into his life, his surroundings, his friends, and you become a complement to his standards and community standing. It is difficulty on many levels:

It is not the expensiveness and fanciness; it is that had you rejected him, you would have been established where you were and had your whole life situated, knowable, and stable where you were if you had not walked away in order to be with him. Maybe your career would have went further if you were not required to cancel a concert or show or meeting in order to be there for his birthday and arrange his party.

CHANGING LAWS

If you want to change the laws in your State, many women will be grateful. It is more difficult for women to fight against falling into poverty than men because women are made differently. The matter is not only the capacity to have children. Women normally have a stronger attachment to their children that were literally "attached" inside of them for nine months so women feel greater responsibility and higher obligations in life.

Getting your State to have a minimum settlement whether or not a prenuptial agreement is made, should be an easy process. You may argue first the Constitutional preamble off the top: Your right as women to form a more perfect "family" union, establish justice (leaving no one out of the joint investment period in life and family), insure domestic tranquility for the children (the making of a smoother transition if the marriage does not last until death), promote the general welfare of all concern as well as of the State that is not suddenly burdened with surges of families being abandoned and or filing for welfare due to lack of a planning prepost-marital arrangement, and to secure the blessings of liberty to ourselves and our posterity (in that easier transitions mean fewer social problems forming for individuals and for the State system).

You may argue second off the top, the Nineteenth Amendment of the Constitution for the right to vote not given to women until 1920. Basically, society and societal institutions formed mainly by men for their conveniences without incorporation and consideration of the conveniences of women.

Obviously, women are not thought of when you have tons of employers easily and readily providing thousands of parking spaces for inanimate cars to sit but then become apprehensive and obtuse when you inquire about a daycare kindergarten for a fellow human being in the stage of childhood as we all were once.

Obviously, women are not thought of when the State legal age for marriage is 16 years old but high schools yet in this year, do not have available an onsite daycare so that our daughters education remain uninterrupted if she gets lured in by a boy before marriage. After all, education remains uninterrupted for the male counterpart. Some states have gun laws in the way of their dads using a shotgun to hunt for the boy as it used to be the norm. Mothers have to now get the adjustment done in our education system.

Our 16-year-old daughters over the years have been forced to drop-out or forced into special programs or otherwise shafted out of an equal education. It is not a single-person matter such as drug use or alcohol. Two persons were involved in the conception of the child, therefore girls should not be placed in straits to abort or to forego education or to live with various men for survival or forced onto a lifetime of welfare for money because of our disorganized American society that continues to be slow in giving women a vote [a say-so] in a society that marginalizes instead of normalizing the conveniences of women and their children.

Every employer that has a parking area for a car, should likewise have a daycare kindergarten to benefit single mothers AND single fathers. Knowing one's child is onsite, moreover, makes for a better worry-free dedicated time-committed employee that does not have to leave the premises early or disappear for part of the day. It is not rocket science. It is long overdue. CEOs that will not facilitate a daycare are pretentious as if they are aliens that are not subject to reproduction. Every manager, boss, and employee is subject to reproduction. It is natural. Those two points of contention gives you as women, a real voice in your State to change the laws, business, and institutions where you live.

CONSEQUENCES OF PASSIVITY

Once you are established where he is, being suddenly displaced and left with nothing when you had something, is to be defrauded. His arrogance will say that he made your life better. That is false.

He made it 'look' better, he did not make it better. Do you know how you play cards and everyone places their money on the table or watch or whatever they have, the round goes well, but at some point one person grabs the money and goods that belong both to him and to everyone at that table, places it in his pocket, invests it in *his* pocket and walks away.

Whatever you had, he did not replace, he took out from you when he <u>acquired you</u> and then he wants you to sign an agreement to sit later at the table with nothing when that is *not* how you came to the table. That is not a game you want to play with your life. You want your stuff back with interest. You want your time and energy back for the years invested. What you came to the table with got invested into his estate though he tries to shame you at the point of breaking up.

What is your estate: your estate albeit your looks, your talents, did promote his enterprise, his position, and his image in the public limelight and among his competitors, colleagues, and fellow tycoons. You are an acquired asset to his branding, his cause, or to his league.

Being a new draw of favorable attention to his image as you and your beauty or your smarts are accompanying him means he is capitalizing on your bosom and or your brain.

Your estate albeit the costs of previous university education and experiences that he found so interesting to commiserate with and to be occupied with as well went into his estate. You are a new condition to his established state of being (estate).

Your estate albeit your intellectual capital which you did input into his life, his endeavors, his concerns, his upsets, and his considerations did as well go into his estate.

You could have fed your time and talents into a corporation or into a go-go club and had a full return on your investment (left with much more than you came in with without any argument). When you arrive to dance go-go with just $5 in your pocket, you do not contract to leave with the $5 or less. You leave with your worth. The enterprise made money while you were there, go-go fans poured in, you had fans and pleased favorites, so you made money and you leave with a lot more money (unless you are a drug user).

ASSESS YOUR VALUE

Do not underestimate yourself or let him erode your brain by telling you that you came in with nothing and are leaving with nothing. Neither did he come in with what he has now when the truth is that you have been part of his upgrade, update, and peace. Tell him you left attending to what was yours to attend to what is his and "ours". It means you invested your chips into whatever was going on with him. In being asked to get out, you need a return on not only your initial investment but years of investing there. He does not have the right to withhold both his share and your share and live in it all while you and the children go out with nothing. You came in with your life not just money. Moreover, during the relationship, you built into the estate alongside with him.

In fact, if you were not there on day eight hundred and fifty five to answer the phone, he would not have been cast in the blockbuster film that brought in millions. When he was hung over and you pushed him out of the door after serving him a cup of coffee, he was able to go the meeting in which he signed a multi-million dollar contract. Without you, he would not have obtained millions of dollars for him for the next few years.

He should think about those things before throwing shade at you about being in his life —making it better and complete. There were days that 'good thing' *you* were not drunk nor high nor hung-over nor shacking but instead were home and could answer a phone or take a message because you certainly did save his butt. You were not there as a silly party whore but you were committed to the process of the business of being his wife and running the household in as much part was your part. You did intervene for him at times and you did mediate some things for him. You got him off of his ass more than one time. Get his mind straight on it all. He should not be talking to you just any kind of way and treating you any kind of way. You were there; you took care of business, crime, and whatever was going on.

You did not come into his life pushing a shopping cart on the street. You have swag-value to factor in. You were what he needed at the time. You are not a nobody. You are not trash nor garbage. You are a person and you have value that is at all times to be respected including before, during, and especially for your sake after. What is yours beforehand was about to be sucked into what is his because <u>your time and presence has mostly left what is yours so he can have good times with you and be with you to enjoy what is his.</u>

Whatever you came in with as yourself and or with an estate and or opportunity venture and or talent, he liked, he loved, he married, and he flourished. You were not living in his closet under the rug; he <u>was</u> capitalizing off of whatever you were and are.

He may have went after you because you were the best go-go dancer and all the other guys wanted you but he got you. Guys go after big fish. You may have been the smartest chick in the room and that is a turn on for him and that is what he acquired and capitalized on.

You may have the "right father" or "right connection" to move his career ahead in banking or in Hollywood or wherever. It may be the expectation of his law firm or political group that he presents himself as a family man and you were conveniently acquired so he can look 'the part', promotable and promising in *their* eyes; love for you is not required just 'use' of you and your willingness to say "yes, I'll marry you".

It is not that you were running his business but you were sustaining the runner running his business which is himself. Your emotional, psychological, educational, intellectual, passion, looks, thoughts, support, encouragement, fed into everyday life at his estate that he back then wanted you to think of as "ours" and that his doing well and being well was "good for *both* of us". If it was "good for both of us", then "both of us" should be able to walk away further along than where we started.

THINKING ABOUT YOURSELF

When you meet the pre-nuptial guy insisting upon it, do not consider it distrust or a blow of hate or shame, consider it a negotiation for how you need to come out of the deal if the relationship breaks up. <u>You are taking off from your current life,</u> you are taking off from other options called the economies of choice, whatever promotional track you were on, whatever safe stable community you were established in. <u>You are now leaving from investing there in your own things to investing in him and with him for a number of years where he lives his life.</u>

Grab an accountant to valuate you –your college education (you do not speak jibberish and you are not influencing him into drugs but you have an upward rising brain functioning on his behalf); your skills; your abilities; experiences; your cooking and hospitality levels because: you will be hosting his clients –in Hollywood even his friends are clients (a good wife helps deals to close); you will be hosting his friends (a good wife makes her husband great and look good); you will be hosting his family (a good wife makes things work as best as she can and tolerates a lot of shit often from his crappy family that pretends to be nice *during* the marriage); you will be hosting his press which gains him double the media coverage and mention (a good wife speaks well of her husband, his talent, what he is doing, and represents him in addition to herself).

Add to that, references from others that have previously capitalized from your presence (former employers); your smile value; your gracious and etiquette value; your beauty value both as a model (get an industry quote) and as porn (get an industry quote if you want); your sensual investments (pole dancing, performance improvements you have acquired in life to satisfy a guy) —the guy is not getting years of an 'ice princess' or a 'wet mop'; your income; your properties; all that you have; your beauty investments including surgeries. Getting larger boobs at his request is a health risk and requires maintenance. Make sure there is a maintenance buffer in the agreement in case something goes wrong with the boobs after you break up and you need repair.

Have the accountant add to that as well your connections such as being the niece of a Senator or of a businessman or government worker in the business license granting department, or your connection to any famous person of any sort. Guys that like to status climb will often marry the girl with the "right father" or "right look for the role of wife" in the industry/business or the right investments in a particular industry, so please calculate that in.

Make a complete assessment of what you know and who you know that may come into play during the relationship with the pre-nup guy.

Once you have a starting point value of what he picked-up on the first date, have the accountant factor in the average length of a marriage to the type of person you are marrying and to place a monetary investment value (any long term investment is similar to a 10-year bond investment or more).

Then tell the accountant to value and forecast his monetary condition and position with and without you. You get the point. Assess, compound, value, forecast, in that you are *going in with this guy* for a few years and trusting him to do the right things including being faithful/including not becoming a drug addict/including not screwing up the marriage. Protect yourself against feeling cheated at the end of the marriage.

Value & Expectations

1. Not all rich men hire house cleaners, cooks, nannies, drivers, personal assistants, gardeners, and butlers. So are any of these roles expected of you to some degree? Add it to your willingness and capability to do these things to your value as a wife.

2. Are you a good cook or good childcare attendant or do you keep

your home better than he keeps his home? Add the degree of quality in action to your value as a wife.

3. Will your appearance and or demeanor and or interest open doors for him —making him more acceptable with his boss or corporate culture or celebrity culture? Add the degree of cooperation with his professional needs to your value as his wife.

4. Will he require you to continue taking birth control pills or other devices during the marriage? It matters because most women hope to relieve their bodies of chemical altering since continuing to take birth control pills after you have a husband and home prolongs the health risk to you. You are increasing your risk for cancer for his sake and you are risking not being able to conceive a child when he is ready or when you remarry. Add the degree of your cooperation with his long-term planning or his

short-term budget into your value to him as his wife.

Why would you consider his budget that he uses to constrain you from furthering family life after marriage? Simple. Some men graduate school or reach another level in their profession and divorce the wife of their hardships in exchange for a younger wife, a blonder wife, a utopia wife (utopia means one that does not remind him of memories of yesteryear nor that tells him to be more appreciative of her), or a trophy wife. You were 'on hold' in all things for him; however he does not later reward you financially nor pay you back nor allow you to enter into the fruits of relief and the fruits of success. He is not there anymore.

5. Do you have professional credentials or any other special intelligence? Remember to include it in your value as his wife since he does expect a certain level of

conversation with you, he does expect to rely on you to step in when and if needed, and he does expect you to fuel his passion for his life and his work.

6. Do you have sexual intensity? Add it to your value as his wife. It does take time, effort, planning, money, to offer sexual variety. It is easier to be a single entertainment once or twice a week. However when married – it all costs more financially and personally—keeping up the amusing behaviors, sleeping in damaging full make-up every night, constant damaging hair styling. All is more challenging. A visiting audience is always easier than a live-in audience asking if you washed his socks, if you fed the dog, why did you take a nap, iron his shirt for tomorrow and is dinner ready yet. Demand remains although there are new daily household obligations expected to be done with no days off.

7. Does he need a lot of attention and approval? If he expects you to mainly focus on him, you do it at the expense of yourself and the children. Basically, you are doing what a mistress does but she does not have burdens whereas you do have other duties, financial matters, self-neglect, children's needs, household matters, that sit on your mind. However, some men do say to their wives to leave all things to someone else so the wife is free to cater and care just for him even in simplest matters like knowing his schedule and greeting him at the door every night with a kiss 365 times a year. Again, you are letting him be more of himself and to have the tilt in the relationship, add that to your value as his wife and do not forget what is going out the door as far as loss and expense.

If a divorce happens, you would have had a great marriage but you would have missed a lot of key moments with your children, you may have missed some of the self-development that occurs when you work as well. You may find yourself further behind in life than you thought would happen; so you need to ensure finances will follow you out of the marriage so you can get grounded again into your own life.

WHAT DO YOU NEED

What do you need to come out with without wiping out the whole store? Do you intend to stay in the community that your investment and faith in him brought you into or if it does not work out, would you then want to be established somewhere else?

Maybe the pre-nuptial at minimum includes a house in the same community or your selected community with all expenses, taxes and maintenance covered on the property forever because it is a house now divided by divorce so two houses in the same town are required. If he can afford several homes including one or two overseas, clearly he can afford one for you in the same neighborhood which is also convenient for co-parenting of the children. Make sure it is security of you as well after the children are gone and the homes have sentimental value.

This looks at sustainment not necessarily income but do add a percentage of income (a return on your investment in him and his life). The percentage can be 'made-up' from the percentage his estate/income did grow during the marriage or just the amount that you normally spent in a year that is fairly average for women in your arena.

The most important thing is that everyone knows where things stand at the end of the road if there is an end of the road.

His family cannot screw you over if he dies or gets in an accident. You get sustainment if you get a family lawyer to set it up jointly <u>NOT</u> one-sided. And his family cannot treat you as trash just because there is a pre-nuptial (especially if you change the law in your State).

If you had not been in that handsome guy's life, especially if he is high status, high powered, over scheduled or truly in fame, by the stress of it all, he might have long ago committed suicide, failed in career and went out of the world altogether.

His family did not climb in bed with him after a business or game or movie failure, you did. He was still sexy in failure or failing health. You were the one egging on his emotional, psychological and life recovery and for him to kickass as a performer or sports star. You were his rock and his soft place to fall. Do not let *his people* write you off as if you are nothing. You are keeping that guy alive. You are completing him just like he is completing you. Do not let him portray a lie.

If you sign a pre-nuptial of nothing after you left your 'entire world that at least somewhat worked out for you', it does stay in the back of your mind. You might not become the best wife with an empty pre-nuptial hanging over your head. You may be passive aggressive to an extent – that means an involuntary helper in the ending of the marriage. This is due to the fact that he feels free and secure but you do not feel secure at all and you are forced to hang on every upset in the household as a threat to your whole life.

It is better for you both if stable footing is already established in a pre-cut non-revocable post-marriage arrangement. It gives him rest and it gives you rest so you both can be actually fully *in* the marriage and in enjoyment of it without nearing a steep cliff every time there is a heated argument and threat of divorce.

If you did not or if you were not invested in yourself, in your being, in your life, then it is likely that he would <u>not</u> have noticed you nor dated you nor asked for your hand in marriage. OPEN your eyes to the reality that you are substantial value on your own. Go into a relationship knowing that. Experts say a relationship though romantic is a lot of business.

If you cannot get along in business, you are likely to divorce. Daily interaction has business in it and there is no escaping the fact. It has dependencies upon each other. It has expectations of contributions. It is business that makes the marriage work (coordinating of intent and mission and time, doing the best things for the best outcome, minding expenses and quality, meeting the needs and wants of each other, re-assessing each other's needs and wants during season changes within the marriage and meeting those new needs in making up the difference, and so forth).

If you were an unruly obscene monster, he would not have likely pursued and acquired you for his estate. YOU ARE ADDING VALUE AND ARE VALID AS A PERSON THERE.

Of course, outright marriage is best and every State should have sustainment safeguards so that there are no sudden wards of the State. Pre-nuptial is not a great way to go into a marriage. I think rebranding it as PrePost-Marital Agreements (PPMAs) is the best way to go as discussed in an earlier Chapter. The agreement should be with included margin for whatever matters such as children or disability or infidelity. Maybe an A, B, C, levels of sustainment post marriage options devised and made part of the license by the State is best to benefit both the State and the couples.

The mandate is a good net to prevent wards of the State due to someone's inability to keep a marriage of his choice together and to stay committed to his own spouse and children.

Having a PrePost-Marital Agreement before getting married is a thousand times more likely to cause that marriage to stay together forever than using a dog chaining pre-nuptial. The dog chaining pre-nuptial introduces fear into having contact and honesty with the person you are marrying. It does not make sense. You both fear marriage seasons of change already.

KNOWING WHAT HE THOUGHT WHEN HE ASKED YOU TO SIGN

He thought a pre-nuptial would ease his mind but after the honeymoon, the pre-nuptial starts to 'bake his noodle' meaning it begins to eat at his brain. He starts to think that you might just be putting up with his crap and hanging on because you really care about the Jaguar he bought you and the expensive rose garden outside and NOT himself. He wonders why you have not stormed out. Then he figures that you do not want to risk access to the shiny stuff not that you actually want the relationship with him.

Therefore, he starts down the path of stupidity in pushing boundaries, pushing your buttons, and pushing to see how much he can get away with while you hang on and claim love.

Under a pre-nuptial, he cheated knowing you would not leave because of the risk to you. He is not happy with his cheating nor with your lack of reaction since you are deemed paralyzed by the fear inducing pre-nuptial. That is just a preview of the stupidity running wild in his head.

He thinks—is it love or is it money? — when really you could have stayed home with your own life instead of trusting him and his sanity to last long enough to keep a happy marriage.

According to him, he does not know if you love him pass his faults or if you are just in motions because you agreed to stay on with the rest of the stuff he has acquired. Note how the rich guy has screwed his own brain over.

Now, he becomes passive aggressive or even aggressive trying to see if you really love him or if it is just the fear of being left with nothing. Self-doubts about himself nearly kill him or cause him some demented insanity.

By the time he finishes being abusive and practicing infidelity to the extent that he wanted, which is for you to decide to leave even at the risk of having nothing (a test of your integrity), you now have a Case that supersedes the pre-nuptial. He brought the fear of doling out money upon himself by dwelling in the fear that he is not really lovable. So now you actually hate him and now he has to dole out money and estate et al to you and a bunch of lawyers that he did not plan on in the middle.

A smart lawyer will then capitalize upon that and hammer out an even much much larger settlement for you. In planning for the end with a biased, unethical, inhumane, disrespectful pre-nuptial agreement, he alone brought about the end of the marriage.

As the Perfectionist woman, if you do not have an accountant at this time, ask a friend to work out the details for you. Make a copy. Run it by some other lawyers and take their advice (there are paid and free consultations with plenty of divorce lawyers and specialized divorce firms even though you are marrying not divorcing).

Afterwards, you yourself take his pre-nuptial paperwork he presented to you and add your paperwork of valuations and estimates and give it to an outside third-party lawyer to balance the two agreements and merge them into one. Do not just blindly sign what he gives you.

At the end of the process, *both he and you need to sign prior to the wedding ceremony.* Once signed, you can make use of the 72-hour grace lemon law by taking it on another consult with a divorce attorney to make sure it is binding on both parties and fair mainly to you and children that may be a part of the break-up.

WHY YOU *AS A WOMAN*, MAY *WANT* A PRE-NUPTIAL AGREEMENT

If you are an a middle-aged woman that has acquired for yourself and your children by hard work, by sacrifice or by a previous marriage, you should consult an investigator to see if he tends to overly mismanaged money and has perpetual lawsuits [incidents such as education loans or a bankruptcy are not problematic but were to solve a problem; you are looking for chronic financial abuse, negligence and irresponsible behavior] and a lawyer for the following reasons:

One. Some wealthy men owe or will owe back taxes that when discovered may jeopardize your assets along with his.

Two. Some wealthy men purchase added items that are not disclosed to you but that are *in your name* upon which it may be later found that *you* owe or are liable for money concerning the purchase if you were married to him at the time.

Three. Some wealthy men are reckless and will gamble any and everything, thereby placing his future, yours, and the children at risk.

Fourth. You do not know if your wealthy man is wealthy or just carries debt well, while he is alive being famous and even pretentiously rich, his name has value and increases the value of every mansion and every item he owns. He is still playing the game. After he dies, vulture creditors swoop in to gather all properties and possessions of his at their peak highest value which are at the sensitive sentimental hours after his death. Before the funeral even starts, you are contacted and your life is being stripped by strangers.

Fifth. He may be wealthy but basically ill-informed of his own wealth and just ignoring of what is happening behind his back or being shaved off the middle.

Sixth. Some men want you to play mommy. He turns his life over and over again and you have to fill in financially every time he quits or has an epiphany –

you do it somewhat out of love but mainly just to survive with some sort stability, consistency and direction. Do not expect that all men have grown up.

Seventh. He may have a financially problematic family. Your Aladdin may have emotional ties with the tales of 40 thieves. This creates problems for the marriage during the marriage and problems for you after the marriage. Eyes open or closed, you may not be the irresponsible one in the relationship; he may be the one.

Eighth. You *may* think the children are key to his not leaving the marriage. But know this, some men live barely knowing they have children. It is you attending to that stuff and *his secretary* attending to that stuff. She/he keeps up with the kids' names, special days, and even shops and chooses *your* kids' gifts out of mid-air. You may be the only person in the relationship spinning around their existence. When you have a Thin Relationship not meaning bad nor unloving but one that involves time away whether nearby in office or far in business travel, it is something to consider. Some relationships work better with the space and it is okay to have one such relationship. Some people are better fueled by the time apart and lightened demands a few days at a time. There are older people that marry but never move out of their separate homes. There is no infidelity. Each person feels secure. There is time in each home. However in your case, be mindful in having forethought about if things do not work out, YOU need to have the children factored in even if you two do not have children yet and *before* divorce or death becomes a reality.

Therefore, it is not an entirely bad idea to nest egg some of your life rewards elsewhere in only your name and irrevocable legal Trust for your survival and the survival of your children to resort to in case of emergency. Some men will support you in that idea and sign a pre-nuptial or prepost-marital agreement that leaves a lot intact for you and untouched.

Ninth. Some men already know that though they are NOT bad cruel guys, they are *NOT* close enough to their money management as to know 100% assuredly what happens if the world collapses, what happens to you, what happens to their own children. Middle managers, family, and accountants do steal and fleece even the most astute of businessmen, celebrities, performers, Wall Street bankers, and so forth. The multitudes of companies and involvements do sniff out blood cents when the chips fall and are without respect of the deceased or the disabled. No one will tell the guy upfront because leaving any issue or cost outstanding until the guy's death increases the monetary value of his stuff which is a greater return on investment or claim capitalized upon by his death.

It is unfortunate but you should weigh not necessarily just the small scope of 'you against me' with your soon-to-be husband as to how both of us will come out if things go that way but also 'WE against the world'. How can "WE" set up things so we are both absolutely sure, everybody —us and the children will be alright come hell or high-water, divorce or death or debt or dismemberment or disability.

His "nice, sweet" family may change gate codes and door locks two minutes after your husband is in a car accident so that you can do nothing not even re-enter to get your own mother's pendant that you sometimes wear. You are worth more respect than that and you need to <u>secure that respect in a contract</u>. You are weeping with no one to weep with you. Vultures do not sit down nor take time nor place into their regard.

They will disrespect you, the children of both of you, and your husband, and they will disrespect and dishonor him and his wishes and words in a heartbeat. I've seen it; I know it. So draw lines in cement ahead of time. Whatever he wants to part to his sister or brother-in-law or mother should be already parted out of his estate and out of his life so that the sister and brother-in-law and mother <u>do not need to step on you at all</u> and disgrace the family and disgrace the family name and disgrace your husband's wishes.

Make sure those sharing the mansion, have their own homes to go home to somewhere even if just the groundskeeper is living there miles out of the city. Mandate in writing that they depart the mansion upon tragedy and or death in order to give you space to sort things out as his wife. Invite who *you* want of his family afterwards—maybe a great uncle a thousand miles away. Make sure the longtime freeloaders have no claims to what you and your husband share or even to just your clothing, jewelry, and bar of soap.

You would be surprised at how pathetic and low-level these things go at the worst possible time and with not one tear shed by them. His own family will start telling you what they *really* thought of him that whole time; they will say "he was shit" and then tell you to "fuck off".

Dealing with the blow of death or dismemberment is bad enough without his crazed family members confiscating and destroying your whole life instead of comforting you as a member of his life — his wife to whom he joined himself <u>in one being</u>.

Do not be greedy nor grabby but be considerate, wise, and weighing of everyone especially those more important or more instrumental in his life should you have to make decisions whether during or insisting before the marriage, navigating during the marriage, or working out details after tragedy. You cannot live with him as his 'guest' and then suddenly know the right decisions to make as his wife. Be his wife. Look out for the honor of his memory. Make sure there is a sense of structure. Make sure that he secures everyone in their zone in writing because otherwise, they will say that 'he said later blah, blah' so they can steal.

In one case, had the wealth went to one child, it would have been honorably spread to all three by purchasing each what he or she valued most and could esteem in honor of the deceased father forever. But instead the wealth went to a child-thief that disrespected the father and did not even invite the father to his wedding, and he kept ALL the wealth to himself and wasted it; basically, calling it justice for himself because at an incident 50 years earlier he did not like his father, as a teen he did not invite his father to his wedding for the same earlier incident and though he was cordial to his father until his death, he still did not like his father. Therefore, he blasted his father's memory even before the wake and again before the funeral and again before the body was in the ground. He made sure to burden and afflict the whole family with his one tale of woe and that stealing all his father's money was justified. He did not even want to pay for his father's funeral though he attended and bitched and moaned to the whole family.

Being the wife means that you do not allow your husband to be so disgraced by someone or something as shown above; but that you ensure he and his interest and your interest are legally contracted on paper and carried forth and understood as final. It is best for everyone to be alright the whole way

without any overreach, overlap or potential conflict when the moment really calls love, comfort, honor, grace and time.

IF YOU GO GAY MATRIMONIAL

Although you appear same sex, one is likely slightly more maternal than the other. Talk to each other and find out if a) one is desperate to have children so much that he/she cannot function because it is 'life purpose and the dream'; b) one has a huge family and prefers a complex people populated existence in house and is mindful of everyone; c) one comes from a huge family and cannot stand it; d) one is more often forgetful and insensitive during the week [the one that closes the door and does not hear anyone come in and perhaps not particularly intrigued if someone does].

These considerations will hopefully lead you to discover which one is more in the maternal identifier role. Generally, the person further away that is more overview, broad and structuring as in the one that wraps the band around the house to make it a quality place doing what it is supposed to do in getting children started and capable in their lives, is more a paternal identifier. The one lighting up the inside of the house and sticking fresh-baked cookies in your face and mindful if your sweater is adequate, leans in the maternal identifier. A child knows which parent always says "run faster" and which parent always says "be careful".

You have watched two parents or people in general for your whole life at home and on television and over the house of your friends, so there is gravity. Just like there is gravity to rock-and-roll.

If you both have morphed into the same person, take a vote by asking your friends which one they want to call when they are crying over a disaster. One person is always more receptive than the other. Perhaps, they call the other person about a flat tire or their screw-up boss.

Nonetheless, divvy it out for better planning purposes so that if the relationship ends, both will come out happier instead of feeling cheated, ignored, and disrespected. Trust me, at the end of a relationship, people grab and go after what they do NOT want and do NOT have the patience for just out of strange alien impulses.

One person takes away the album collection of the other person but has no record player and really has no interest in the inconvenience of looking for an album and playing one when he/she can just speak outloud and hear a selection from Alexa or Siri or some other home system. The other person actually swaddles albums in cloth and spends all afternoon cleaning them. It would cruelly hurt to be in deprivation –to reach out and the collection is not there for care. One person wants to divide the microbrewery. The person hates beer and truly prefers wine but for some reason wants the microbrewery or wants it sold for money not needed from it.

Before divorce aliens take over your relationship and while you are in love and settled, no matter what you think, figure out towards each other's life happiness in case you divorce each other. It is best for you both. It is best for the children whether natural or adopted. It safeguards what you have as cherished instead of cursed upon separation.

Remember you both went in alright and you both have to decide, plan and make sure that if things do not stay the same then you both will go out alright. What is special stays special forever for both of you.

After you articulate guaranteed protections for you, your partner, and the children in a pre-nuptial or prepost-matrimonial agreement, so a third-party cannot go in and challenge your estate, you need to know one thing.

If the Supreme Court decision is overturned or your State makes a different law, your nuptials are still protected under common law as long as you two are competent, mature in age, and human and have annexed yourselves to each other (mixed estates, joint accounts, living in one household). Common law is non-traditional without the force of religion nor sudden religious conversion and without changing religion nor definitions and is the Constitutional provisional allowed for those taking nuptials not according to religious traditions, approvals, and formula. The government will not make your spouse go away nor attempt to ungay you.

Although cake is not part of this, you do know that all bakeries cannot be expected to cover all events but you will find one. For two diabetics to get married, it is a real cake hunt to find a bakery that makes a diabetic wedding cake —in case you have never been in that situation. Not everyone does Greek weddings, not everyone does Italian weddings, nor Jewish weddings, and being able to upsell can determine acceptance as a client, so you can expect to be in a cake hunt whether gay or straight, diabetic or healthy. Do not take it personally. But be confident in America, you will always find what you are looking for. Do not let it rain on your own parade which is your special day. Do not stress; society does adjust in time. You will be okay. Everything will be fine.

Our primary concern here is that you sort through the pre-nuptial though you may not need it in the future. Install love and light upfront and then drop it. Both of you have to be alright in the end if things do not work out. It is love to make sure.

LEAPING TOGETHER

Being Pro+Life means knowing your worth.

The Proverbs 31 woman is a whole woman, is a whole person, whether in a marriage or without a marriage.

Keep your own goal of heading toward a good life for yourself and your children. Do not bargain away your own reality for any reason. Seldom do things zip right into a great place after a divorce or death. Address reality in thinking of yourself and on another day, address reality as a couple.

All sides need to know that everyone will be okay whether together or apart *before* going into the marriage. All doors are open and this is the best time to put into writing what happens when we are together and what happens if we fall apart.

SUMMARY

Love going in, love during, and love after no matter what; that is how the marriage part of our lives is to happen.

Make sure you speak to your beloved and that both of you speak to a family lawyer chosen jointly to ensure everyone comes out alright if things fall apart. It is a duty of love.

Marriage is forever whether you stay married or not. The individual you have chosen *stays* incorporated into your life and you stay incorporated into his. You will never fully get back the years spent, the location changes, the time, the effort, the real money put in, and so on. You will learn to select pieces to cherish, honor, and respect. You will not be able to undo the children nor that section of your life. Marriage is as all other adventures in your life that involves your soul.

To keep decency as much as possible, be realistic about the 'just in case' scenario. If you get a certain thing like a house or a car or an apartment or a really great job and you think it is the last one; sometimes it is not. You may have to go onto another whether it is a matter of your need or your want or a miscellaneous incident or the hurricane that collapsed it and made it unlivable.

In life, there are starts and restarts throughout just like a plant sheds leaves during a season or has those leaves cut off but still yet it goes on in progress and in process of shooting forth new growth from its center. The plant is not disappointed, discouraged, but has faith of life going on and not being left empty.

The plant's life cannot "park" in one situation and neither can your life "park" in one situation.

You will continue to grow up and to grow out, your partner will continue to grow up and to grow out, and your life together will continue to grow up and to grow out whether together or apart.

That means you can count on adjusting during the marriage, changing routines as things progress, reevaluating what is needed and navigating role changes and amounts of effort by everyone involved. And now, you know not to resent those normal typical contortions of that which moves forward and re-stabilizes (new settled routine) each time for you both and for the quality of survival and quality of life for you both.

If there is the possibility of children whether natural or adopting or of third party interference (extended family, business, assholes, lawyers), you should legally plan in writing how your lives will work out if after incorporating your lives together, you have to pull out and pull it apart again in becoming two divorcees.

Since both are invested in the marriage, both are leaving in some other condition, it should be no problem in applying the love and care now to guarantee that both come out well with a return on investment for the sake of lasting life peace and any children that come along.

Therefore, never will arguments nor the marriage hang on things. Arguments and the marriage instead will hang on love, and choice and respect. Doubts and suspicions will have no place because both know the end from the beginning and both choose love now and are fully present in the marriage.

Disclaimer: This publication is designed to provide general counseling information in regard to the subject matter covered. It is sold with the understanding that the publisher or writer is not engaged in tendering legal, accounting, or other professional service. If legal advice or other expert assistance is required, the services of a competent professional person should be sought.

Develop a greater sense of Happiness in your life.

Be sure to join us on https://www.twitter.com/happinessgoal

Buy this 1891 Western adventure selection for your children (ages 12 to 19) or buy copies for your class. A very interesting book your youth will enjoy.

An 1891 Western

Dead Man's

Curve

EDGAR O. SMITH

Order Yours Today!

It is rumored that a second book is in the works.